BRITANNICUS

PLAYS BY HOWARD RUBENSTEIN

AGAMEMNON by Aeschylus, translated with reconstructed stage directions

BRITANNICUS by Jean Racine, translated and adapted

BROTHERS ALL

THE GOLEM, MAN OF EARTH

TONY AND CLEO

THE TROJAN WOMEN by Euripides, translated and adapted in response to Aristophanes' and Aristotle's criticism of Euripides

Also by HOWARD RUBENSTEIN

MACCABEE, an Epic in Free Verse

BRITANNICUS

A Play in Two Acts

Adapted from
Jean Racine's *Britannicus*

by

HOWARD RUBENSTEIN

Granite Hills Press™

BRITANNICUS
A Play in Two Acts
Adapted from
Jean Racine's *Britannicus*
by Howard Rubenstein

Published 2009 by Granite Hills Press™

SAN 298–072X

Cover by Chuck Conners. Front cover photograph by Howard Rubenstein 2008: *Marble portrait bust of a young man, possibly a member of the Julio-Claudian Imperial Family* (possibly Britannicus), early first century, the Ancient Agora Museum of the Stoa of Attalos, Athens. Back cover cyberwatercolor by Chuck Conners based on a painting by John William Waterhouse.

Cataloging in Publication
  Rubenstein, Howard S. 1931–
    Britannicus : a play in two acts adapted from Jean Racine's
    Britannicus / by Howard Rubenstein;
      p. cm
      LCCN: 2009900121
      ISBN-13: 978-1-929468-14-0
      1. French–Drama. 2. Roman–Drama. 3. Historical–Drama.
        4. Tragedy–Drama.
    I. Jean Racine
    II. Title

Printed in the United States of America

To Judy

PREFACE

Britannicus, a play by Jean Racine, one of the three great French dramatists of the seventeenth century, tells the story of the emperor Nero early in his reign when he was still popular with the Roman people and only a "budding monster" (Racine's epithet). The play ends when the bud begins to open. Like many of Racine's plays—eleven tragedies and one comedy—*Britannicus* has a beauty and simplicity of language; a well-constructed and focused plot that flows steadily with suspense, excitement, and irony, to its conclusion; vivid and distinctive characterizations; and a brilliant lucidity.

Few translations of Racine exist in English. The main deterrents to translation have been two: Racine in French was considered "perfect," and the French classical poetic form, the alexandrine, as used by Racine, could not be translated gracefully into English. Alexandrines sound majestic in French, but in English they sound comical, rendering them inappropriate for translations of French tragedy. Racine in effect was "untranslatable." Those who tried to translate him fit their words into English poetic forms, sometimes in imitation of Shakespeare, but there is no evidence that those translations brought admiration to Racine among the English-speaking nations.

I decided to break free of the constraints of Racine's perfection and inimitable poetry and express the play's content in clear, standard American English in free verse. I made other deliberate changes as well. I deleted words and even sentences that have no relevance to a modern audience, and I added words of my own to clarify the characters and the dialogue. I took slight liberties with the story, something Racine himself did in his tragic histories and Euripides-based plays. In the "Second Preface" to *Andromaque*, Racine, probably to shield himself from the critic's attack, wrote, "There is a world of difference between destroying the very foundations of a story and changing some of the incidents. . . . [O]ne must not delight in quibbling [with new playwrights of ancient themes] . . . for the few changes they may have made to the story . . . but rather strive to consider the excellent use they made of those changes, and the ingenious way in which they adapted the story to suit their theme." Racine himself even deleted two passages from *Britannicus* after its first printing. In justifying Racine's revision, one translator noted, "Neither [passage] is significant for the action of the tragedy." Exactly so.

Racine's original play has five acts, each about fifteen to twenty minutes in length, for a total running time of about one hundred minutes. My adaptation has only two acts. Act 1 incorporates Racine's acts 1 through 3 and runs about sixty minutes; act 2 incorporates Racine's acts 4 and 5 and runs about forty minutes; thus, the total running time is again about one hundred minutes. I mention this only because some critics assumed that by reducing the number of acts from five to two, I had discarded three acts to shorten the play. My adaptation of *Britannicus* is not a long play, but it is not shorter than the original.

Purists may object to the things I did. But I did not write my adaptation of *Britannicus* only for them. I wrote it to give a general and modern English-speaking audience access to one of the world's great plays.

Howard Rubenstein

ACKNOWLEDGMENTS

It is a pleasure to acknowledge my indebtedness to the many people who helped me in creating this adaptation from the French of Jean Racine's *Britannicus*. Donald S. Schier, professor of Romance languages at Carleton College in Northfield, Minnesota, introduced me to Racine and *Britannicus* in his class of French language and literature in 1952. Madeleine and René de la Quérière and their four children took me into their home in France during two summers in the 1950s and helped make France and its language and culture real for me.

To adapt *Britannicus*, I used the Racine text established by Paul Mesnard and amended by Raymond Picard (Laurel Language Library [Germaine Brée, General Editor, French Series, Dell, 1963, 1964]). I found three English translations useful: those by Kenneth Muir (Mermaid Dramabook, 1960); Samuel Solomon (Modern Library, 1969); and C. H. Sisson (World's Classics, Oxford, 1987).

Britannicus had its premiere at Compass Theatre (formerly 6th@Penn Theatre), San Diego, on October 23, 2008, produced by Dale Morris and directed by Miriam Cuperman. Stage manager was John Harris, set designer Brian Redfern, costumer designer Abigail Hewes, and lighting designer Mitchell Simkovsky. The cast comprised Glynn Bedington (Agrippina), Rich Carrillo (Nero), Bayardo de Murguia (Britannicus), Jenna Selby (Junia), Neil McDonald (Burrus), Dale Morris (Narcissus), Renée Gándola (Albina), Anthony Hamm (Guard), and William Parker Shore (Guard). I am grateful to the director and the cast for suggesting changes to clarify and improve the script.

I thank Ingar Quist and Rebecca Rauff for editing the final manuscript.

I am most grateful to my wife, Judith, for her assistance in solving difficulties in the French text and for her suggestions, editing, support, and love. Judy also found the bust in the Ancient Agora Museum of the Stoa of Attalos, Athens, identified as early first century *Marble portrait bust of a young man, possibly a member of the Julio-Claudian Imperial Family.* Britannicus is one who fits this description, and my photograph of that bust is featured on the front cover.

Howard Rubenstein
San Diego
March 11, 2009

BRITANNICUS

CHARACTERS

BRITANNICUS. A prince; son of the emperor Claudius and Messalina; brother of NERO's wife, Octavia; stepson of AGRIPPINA; stepbrother and brother-in-law of NERO; fiancé of JUNIA; mid-adolescent. (His name means "Britain vanquished," and he received it because Britain was conquered by Rome at the time of his birth.)

NERO. Roman emperor; son of AGRIPPINA and Domitius Aenobarbus; adopted son of the emperor Claudius; stepbrother and brother-in-law of BRITANNICUS; husband of Octavia; late adolescent.

AGRIPPINA. Mother of NERO; stepmother of BRITANNICUS; widow of Domitius Aenobarbus (father of NERO) and also widow of Claudius (father of BRITANNICUS); middle-aged; matronly, but attractive and seductive.

JUNIA. A princess; descendant of the emperor Augustus; fiancée of BRITANNICUS; mid-adolescent.

BURRUS. Tutor and adviser to NERO; middle-aged.

NARCISSUS. Confidant of BRITANNICUS and informer for NERO; middle-aged.

ALBINA. Attendant of AGRIPPINA; young to middle-aged.

Two Guards. Silent parts.

Scenes: Rome. The atrium of the Palace of the Emperors.

Time: A day in February, 55 CE.
  Act I
      Scene 1:   Middle of the night
      Scene 2:   Dawn
      Scene 3:   Morning
  Act II
      Scene 1:   Early afternoon
      Scene 2:   Late afternoon
      Scene 3:   Evening

PRONUNCIATION GUIDE

Agrippina:	Ag-rip-PEE-nuh
Albina:	Al-BEE-nuh
Britannicus:	Brit-TAN-nick-cuss
Burrus:	BUR-russ
Germanicus:	Jur-MAN-ick-cuss
Junia:	JOO-nee-uh
Messalina:	Mess-uh-LEE-nuh
Narcissus:	Nahr-SIS-suss
Nero:	NEAR-oh
Octavia:	Ahk-TAY-vee-uh
Pallas:	PAL-luss
Silanus:	Suh-LAY-nuss
Tiberius:	Ty-BEER-ee-uss

BRITANNICUS

ACT I

Scene 1

TIME: *A day in February, 55 CE, the middle of the night.*

SCENE: *Rome. The atrium of the Palace of the Emperors. Upstage is a segment of the peristyle—a colonnade of six Doric columns between which, further upstage, may be seen a garden, and beyond the garden a segment of the parallel colonnade. (See back cover.) Entrances and exits take place between the columns, or stage right or left, or through the main aisle of the theater.*

AT RISE: *Torch lamps are burning. AGRIPPINA is pacing anxiously. The sound of marching footsteps approaching is heard. AGRIPPINA hides behind a column. GUARDS enter escorting JUNIA, in a nightgown, frightened. The GUARDS pause momentarily, gaze about, and then decisively exit with JUNIA. AGRIP-PINA emerges from her hiding place.*

ALBINA. (*Enters.*) My lady, why are you here?
Why aren't you in bed?
Why are you awake,
wandering about the palace in the middle of the night,
without attendants?

AGRIPPINA. I cannot sleep!
    I shall wait here all night if I must
    to catch my son when he awakens.
    He has no trouble sleeping—
    Nero, the emperor!—
    but he cares little that his actions
    keep his mother awake!

ALBINA. And what was all that commotion?

AGRIPPINA. Armed guards!
    I saw them with my own eyes—
    dragging the princess Junia here to the palace—
    and at this hour!

    Oh, Albina, now I understand.
    All that I foretold is happening.
    Nero has declared himself against Britannicus.
    The emperor, grown weary of making himself loved,
    now wants to make himself feared!
    And Britannicus stands in his way.
    Well, I can see that it is just a matter of time
    before Nero will turn on me.

ALBINA. My lady, Nero is your son
    and owes you the air he breathes.
    But he owes you more than that.
    It was you who persuaded your husband
    Claudius, the previous emperor,
    to adopt Nero as his son.
    And it was you who persuaded Claudius
    to name Nero his successor
    in preference to his own son, Britannicus.
    My lady, Nero owes you everything.

AGRIPPINA. Nero owes me everything.
    Yes, Albina, that is so.
    But he is ungrateful
    and resents everything I've done.

ALBINA. What makes you say that?
    He appears to do everything you want.
    He has reigned for two whole years,
    and during that time
    he has been a model emperor.
    Rome considers herself
    back in the days of the Republic.
    Everyone says, "Nero, although young,
    rules like a father and has all the virtues
    that Augustus had when old."

AGRIPPINA. That's what people say, Albina,
    but he can't fool me.
    I'm his mother!
    It looks as if the future is about to destroy the past!
    He has the worst characteristics of his father—
    sad one moment, wild the next—
    and all the arrogance of my father's side.

    Tyranny always bears good fruit at first.
    Think of my brother, Caligula!
    He delighted Rome
    until he could no longer contain
    his insane cruelty and fury.
    Then Rome's delight turned to horror.

ALBINA. Well, my lady, Nero doesn't seem
    to be like him at all.

AGRIPPINA. Albina, you see him
    as a *perfect* emperor.
    Well, even if he is,
    did I hand him the tiller of the ship of state
    so that he could please
    only the Senate and the People of Rome?
    Let him be the father of his country!
    But let him never forget
    that Agrippina is his mother!

    I must tell you about the criminal act
    that Nero has just committed
    and that I myself witnessed.

    Nero knows—
    for love cannot remain a secret—
    that the princess Junia,
    who is descended from the emperor Augustus,
    is in love with Britannicus,
    and that Britannicus adores her.
    And yet this very same Nero—
    who you tell me has so much virtue!—
    has had Junia carried from her home
    during the darkest hours of night
    and brought here to the palace!
    What does he want with her?
    Is he doing this for the pleasure
    of hurting them?
    Or to punish me
    because I supported them?

ALBINA. You supported them?
    My lady,
    when did you ever support Britannicus?

AGRIPPINA. Stop it, Albina!
   I confess it was I who ruined Britannicus.
   He, by right, should have had the throne.
   He knows he was cast off because of me.
   And Junia knows what I did
   to her brother, Silanus.
   Claudius intended Silanus as a husband
   for his daughter, Octavia.
   But I prevented the marriage—
   broke the engagement—
   because I wanted Octavia
   for my own son, Nero,
   and Claudius always granted my wishes.

ALBINA. Well, my lady,
   Nero is emperor now.
   His wife, Octavia, is rather timid.
   She doesn't say much,
   and hardly anyone speaks of her,
   even though she is the emperor's wife.
   But Rome and the court speak a great deal
   about the emperor's mother!
   Your name is held as sacred as his own.
   Whenever you appear in public,
   the imperial emblems and laurels
   are held up first to you.
   What further signs of Nero's gratitude
   are you looking for?

AGRIPPINA. Albina, yes,
   Nero gives me many honors.
   But I'd prefer fewer honors
   and more authority.
   Time was I ruled the Senate—

invisible,
but a powerful presence nonetheless.
Nero then was not drunk with greatness.
But one day all that changed,
and he was suddenly dazzled
with his own glory.

ALBINA. I remember that day!
Kings and ambassadors
from many nations
came to pay homage to Nero
as Lord of the Universe.

AGRIPPINA. Yes. I remember that day well!
I was just about to take my place
on the throne beside Nero
when he rose, ran to embrace me,
but then—on whose advice I do not know—
the ungrateful and insolent boy
edged me away from the throne!
Imagine my humiliation!
Since that moment,
my power has dwindled day by day
until now only a shadow remains.

ALBINA. If that is what is troubling you,
why don't you go and talk to him about it?
Otherwise, these thoughts will poison you.
Tell him whatever is on your mind.
Talking to him is the only way
he'll learn what you think
and you'll learn what he thinks—
the only way to assuage your concerns.

AGRIPPINA. But, my dear Albina,
    I am allowed audiences with him—
    my own son!—
    only at fixed times,
    and only with mutual advisers as go-betweens.
    They never let us speak directly to each other.
    Tell me, Albina, is this any way to treat a mother?
    But I intend to pursue him as much as he avoids me.
    That is why I came here—
    to wait for him and catch him!

    (*Seeing* BURRUS *approaching.*)
    But now I may find out
    why the princess Junia
    was kidnapped in the middle of the night,
    and what mischief Nero is planning!

    (BURRUS *enters.*)

BURRUS. My lady, I did not find you
    in your apartments,
    so I came to look for you here.
    By the emperor's command,
    I come to give you information
    about an incident that appears alarming,
    but that came about with due deliberation.
    Nero wishes you to understand that.

AGRIPPINA. So, Caesar is awake now, too!
    Well, if Caesar wants me to understand something,
    take me to him so he can explain it himself.

BURRUS. He is in conference now
    and does not wish to be disturbed.

AGRIPPINA. He's in conference *now!*
    Well then, Burrus,
    perhaps you and I can have a talk.

BURRUS. Certainly, my lady.

AGRIPPINA. Why do you always
    make it so hard
    for me to see the emperor?
    Must I wait all night here
    or crawl on my knees like a beggar
    to talk to him?
    Did I get you your position
    so that you could place a barrier
    between my son and me?
    You dare not leave him alone for a moment,
    and you want him to forget me completely?

BURRUS. My lady . . .

AGRIPPINA. When I selected you as his tutor,
    was it for this—
    for you to control the empire in his name?
    Had I known that your aim
    was to subjugate me,
    I would have left you in the army
    permanently,
    (*Contemptuously.*) to win
    those corroding medals of honor
    the army bestows on heroes
    so readily.

BURRUS. My lady!

AGRIPPINA. Nero is no longer a child.
　　Don't treat him like one.
　　It's time he governed on his own.
　　Or have you decided he must see everything
　　only through your eyes?
　　Wouldn't it be better if he consulted
　　his ancestors—Augustus, Tiberius,
　　or Germanicus, my father?
　　And even though I'm not as great as they,
　　I have something worthwhile to teach—
　　such as keeping one's distance
　　from one's subjects!

BURRUS. My lady, I know it was you
　　who placed the boy Caesar
　　in my care—I, a soldier,
　　with a soldier's love of liberty
　　and honesty.
　　But did I promise to make him
　　an emperor who obeyed only you?

　　My lady, forgive me for saying so,
　　but it's not you to whom I must answer now.
　　It is your son, who is more than a son.
　　He is Ruler of the World!
　　And I am responsible to him and to the empire
　　that he governs.
　　If you wanted him to be educated
　　by panderers or slaves,
　　you could have found thousands—
　　all competing to drag him down.
　　They would have kept him a child
　　forever.

Besides, what is there for you to complain of?
You are revered.
Those who swear by the emperor
also swear by his mother.
True, he does not come by
to see you every day,
to lay the world at your feet.
But should he?
Surely he can show his gratitude
in other ways than dependence on you!
Was it your intention
that he should be Caesar
in name only?

Let me speak plainly.
Rome dates her imperial liberty
from the reign of Nero.
The empire is no longer one man's toy.
The emperor allows free elections.
That is no mean accomplishment.
Think of it!
The magistrates are elected.
And the emperor appoints generals
whom the soldiers like and respect.
It doesn't really matter
what the emperor thinks of us,
so long as our advice leads to his glory,
so long as his reign flourishes,
so long as Rome remains free,
and so long as this beneficent Caesar
continues to hold the power!

Believe me, my lady,
Nero can manage for himself.

Even I obey him more than I advise him.
Don't worry about him.
To do well,
he only has to be allowed to be himself.
Then one good deed will follow another
like links on a shining chain.

AGRIPPINA. Well then, will you,
who has just sung of Nero's many virtues,
explain why he had Junia kidnapped?
Kidnapping is a violent and terrorizing crime,
abominable to all civilized people, is it not?
What is she accused of?
What harm has she done?
Is that young girl an enemy of the state?

BURRUS. That is the very matter
I came to speak to you about.
The emperor has not accused Junia
of any crime.
She is now in the palace of her ancestors,
and she has been given the finest apartments.
You surely know
that through the rights her ancestry grants her,
she might turn her fiancé, Britannicus,
into a rebel-prince.
So you must admit that a descendant of Augustus
should not marry without Caesar's consent.

AGRIPPINA. Now I understand!
Nero is telling me—through you—
that Britannicus cannot count on a choice
I have made.
Nero now seeks to show

that although his mother makes promises,
she cannot keep them!
And although Rome loves me now,
Caesar, by this insult, wishes to change that.
Well, I should like to warn him to take care!
I may have more influence in the empire
than he thinks!

BURRUS. My lady, must you always think
the worst of him?
Blame him for everything?
You cannot possibly think Nero believes
that you are siding with Britannicus—
that you support him against Nero!

AGRIPPINA. No, of course not!
Who in his right mind would want my support
when everyone knows
that Nero banishes me from his presence?

BURRUS. But here comes Britannicus!
I will leave you two alone.

(BURRUS *exits, passing first* BRITANNICUS *and then*
NARCISSUS *as they enter.* BURRUS *salutes* BRI-
TANNICUS *and coolly nods to* NARCISSUS, *who
coolly returns the nod.*)

AGRIPPINA. Britannicus,
what are you doing here?
This court is hostile toward you.
What are you looking for?

BRITANNICUS. *What am I looking for?*
O Jupiter and all the Gods!
Everything I've lost is here!
The princess Junia
was dragged here in the middle of the night,
surrounded by a company of soldiers
threatening her.
Why?
To separate her from me?

AGRIPPINA. I know all about that,
and I feel as if the wrongs against you
have been committed against me.
I have already complained bitterly,
and I'm not going to let the matter drop there.
I intend to do something about it!
But talking here is dangerous.
Let's talk later in my apartments. (*Exits.*)

BRITANNICUS. What do you think, Narcissus?
Can I believe her? Trust her?
Is she going to smooth things over
between Nero and me?
Is this not the same Agrippina
who married my father and then ruined me?
The same Agrippina who—you tell me—
poisoned him, when he was already dying,
to be certain that Death wasn't cheated?

NARCISSUS. My lord, what does it matter
what she did then,
now that she's given you Junia?
So, yes, I think you can trust her.
You both share the same troubles,

so she certainly has
your best interest at heart.

Now, listen to me.
You can't come to the palace
to whimper and whine.
That will only win the court's contempt.
You have to inspire fear.
Otherwise, you will achieve nothing
and be filled with resentment
and go on complaining forever.

BRITANNICUS. I have renounced the empire,
which was mine by right.
And now I'm all alone.
My father's friends treat me like a stranger.
The mere sight of me chills them.
I can see them shudder at a distance,
only to give me a big smile
when they draw near
and tell me how glad they are to see me,
how tall I've grown,
and what a good-looking young man
I've become.
And those who are still loyal to me
have nothing at all to do with me
because they think I'm too young.
So whom do I see surrounding me
but corrupt so-called friends?
They watch my every move,
keep track of my every word.
They're all chosen by Nero as informers.
I'm sold every day.
Nero knows everything I do and plan to do.

Why, Narcissus, he knows my heart
as well as you do!

NARCISSUS. My lord, you have to be
more discreet about choosing friends
and what you tell them.
You can't go around confiding to the world.

BRITANNICUS. You're right, of course.
But I've always had a hard time
hiding my feelings and learning to mistrust.
So I've been deceived and betrayed
on many occasions.

NARCISSUS. That shows you have
a noble and generous heart.

BRITANNICUS. My father, Claudius—
I'll always remember it—said that you,
Narcissus, alone of all his freedmen,
were always loyal and true.
And you have many times saved me from danger.
Find out where Nero holds the princess Junia.
Find out whether she is safe and when I may see her.
In the meantime, I'll go to Agrippina
and listen to her advice,
and perhaps become more of a friend to her
than she wishes.

(*They exit.*)

(*Fade-out.*)

Scene 2

TIME: *Dawn.*

AT RISE: GUARDS *enter, extinguish the torches, and exit.*
NERO *and* BURRUS *enter, conversing.*

NERO. Although she is wrong, Burrus,
      she is still my mother.
      Whoever advises her misadvises her
      by encouraging her whims
      and pouring poison into her ears.
      I suspect it is that insolent minister of hers, Pallas.
      I tell you for the last time, Burrus,
      make sure he's gone from these precincts
      and out of Rome by the end of the day.
      The safety of the empire is at stake.

BURRUS. Yes, my lord.

NERO. You may go now, Burrus.

      (BURRUS *exits as* NARCISSUS *enters. As they pass
      each other, they nod coolly. NARCISSUS stands mo-
      tionless, observing NERO, who, unaware that anyone
      else is present, is pacing, twirling, and sighing. He picks
      up his lyre and begins to play.*)

NERO. (*Singing and playing.*)
      When I saw her tonight,
      I succumbed at the sight!
      Nero is in love.

I tried to speak; my voice did flee!
O Gods in heaven, what's happening to me?
Caesar is in love.

This girl fills me with desire!
My flesh, my heart, my soul's afire!
Nero is in love.

NARCISSUS. My lord, what a lovely song!
    Is it new?

NERO. I just composed it, Narcissus.

NARCISSUS. It's pleasant to hear a song
    about Caesar's love of the Gods.

    Well then, now that you have Junia,
    you are assured of all Rome.
    Your enemies are quite defeated.
    But, my lord, you look troubled—
    more so than even Britannicus.

NERO. Oh, Narcissus!
    It's happened at last!

NARCISSUS. What has happened?

NERO. Nero is in love!

NARCISSUS. *You?* Surely you jest!

NERO. I'm in love, Narcissus!
    I worship Junia!
    I must have her as my wife!

NARCISSUS. (*Astonished.*)
    You love Junia?

NERO. (*Sighing and playing the lyre intermittently.*)
    Last night
    I secretly watched her as she arrived.
    I could see her eyes wet with tears.
    How they shone amid the torches
    and the steel of the swords!
    How beautiful she was,
    even snatched from sleep,
    still in her nightgown!
    The sight of her so affected me
    that when I tried to speak,
    I could not.
    Dumbstruck, I let her pass right by
    as she went to her apartments.
    So I went back to mine
    and crawled into bed,
    where I tried hard not to think of her,
    but in my mind I saw her still.
    The harder I tried to forget her,
    the more vivid she became.
    I loved even the weeping tears I caused.
    I imagined I asked her pardon.
    And so, unable to get her out of my mind,
    I lay there the whole night through,
    my eyes not closing once,
    waiting for the light of morning.

    Perhaps my imagination flatters her,
    and she's not so beautiful after all.
    Narcissus, what do you think?

NARCISSUS. Why has she avoided
   you and the court?

NERO. She blames me for her brother's death.
   And also perhaps
   she wanted to keep her beauty from my sight.
   She's probably still a virgin,
   and virginity in the palace is quite a novelty.
   There's not a woman in Rome
   who's not been made more vain
   after I've made love to her.
   Narcissus, the word's gone out! (*Smiles.*)
   Once a woman is confident of her beauty,
   she can't wait to try it out on me—
   all except Junia.
   She regards such honors as a disgrace.
   She isn't the least bit interested in finding out
   whether Caesar wants to take her to bed,
   or whether he's a good lover,
   or whether there's a special pleasure
   in sleeping with the emperor.
   Tell me, Narcissus,
   does Britannicus love her?

NARCISSUS. You need to ask, my lord?

NERO. But he is so young.
   Does he even know the thrill
   of an enchanting glance
   or an accidental touch?
   Do you think he's even kissed her?

NARCISSUS. My lord, her beauty
   moves him to tears.

And he does whatever she asks.
So have no doubt about it.
Britannicus loves her.
Perhaps he's even persuaded her to . . .

NERO. To . . . what? What are you saying?

NARCISSUS. I don't really know, my lord,
    but I can tell you
    there are times he comes to the palace
    to see you,
    and when his requests are denied,
    he storms out, his heart full of anger,
    bewailing your ingratitude.
    And then he goes to see Junia.
    When he leaves her, he is very happy.

NERO. Too bad for him!
    He would be better off if he displeased her.
    Nero won't endure jealousy
    without revenge!

NARCISSUS. I don't think you have
    cause for concern, my lord.
    Britannicus is probably the only one
    whom Junia has ever cared for,
    and she probably pities him
    more than she loves him.
    It is his tears she responds to.
    But now you have the opportunity
    to open her eyes—
    to let her see at close quarters
    all of Caesar's splendor!

My lord, when she sees you
wearing the emperor's crown,
and in all your glory,
and you sigh to her
that she's captivated you completely,
you have only to command her to love you,
and she will love you.

NERO. It won't be as easy as you think,
    with everyone against me.

NARCISSUS. *Everyone?*

NERO. Everyone—Agrippina, Octavia, Burrus,
    and all of Rome.
    And I can't disregard
    my past years of beneficent reign.

    As for my wife, Octavia, I feel nothing,
    and I should be only too happy for a divorce
    to lift the yoke that was imposed on me.
    Even the Gods condemn her.
    She has been unable to conceive,
    and so she prays to them,
    but they do not answer her prayers.
    And the empire wants an heir.

NARCISSUS. Well then,
    why not divorce her right away?
    Augustus divorced
    to marry his adored Livia.
    And it was from that union,
    arising from divorce,
    that you inherited the empire.

You owe it to yourself and Rome
to do the same!

NERO. My mother arranged my marriage,
and she is implacable.
Can't you see her, eyes blazing,
bringing Octavia to me,
and declaring that a marriage arranged by her
is sacred and indissoluble?
And striking ever sharper blows
on my soul,
calling me an ungrateful son?
I can't begin to imagine
her torrent of endless cries.

NARCISSUS. Are you not, my lord,
your own master—and hers, too?
Are we always to see you cowering before her
and doing exactly as she bids?
Live and reign for yourself—not for her!
Are you afraid of her?
You needn't be.
You just banished her adviser, Pallas,
for his impudence,
in spite of her fondness for him.

NERO. I hear your advice
and know that it is good.
And when she's not around,
I'm quite capable of giving orders
and even making threats.
But only after I've worked myself into a frenzy
am I able to defy her.
As soon as I see her, I become powerless.

Those eyes of hers!
For so many years I've looked to them
to learn what I must do!
And I cannot forget
that everything I have I owe to her.
Hard as I try,
my will is powerless before hers.
I tremble before her!
It is to free myself from this dependence
that I avoid her as much as I can.
And I deliberately offend and provoke her
to make her run away from me.

But we must not stand here and talk.
Britannicus may see us
and suspect your loyalty.

NARCISSUS. Don't worry about him!
Britannicus trusts me completely!
He thinks I'm seeing you now at his command
to find out how things are going for him.
He wants to know your most secret thoughts
through my lips
and, above all, to see his beloved Junia again.
He expects my help in that matter.

NERO. And he shall have it, Narcissus!
He shall have it.
Take him the good news.
Soon he will see her.

NARCISSUS. (*Puzzled.*) My lord,
I don't understand.

NERO. I have my reasons, Narcissus,
    and Britannicus will pay dearly
    for the pleasure of seeing his beloved again.
    Be sure to boast to him
    how cleverly you arranged it . . .
    and how, for his sake, you deceived me . . .
    and that he will be seeing her
    through no wish of mine.
    But hush! Here she is.
    Go and find Britannicus
    and bring him here.

    (NARCISSUS *exits, bowing to* JUNIA *as she enters.*)

JUNIA. (*Startled on seeing* NERO.) My lord,
    I was on my way to see Octavia,
    not the emperor. (*Turning to go.*)

NERO. Stay!

    (JUNIA *stops and turns to face him.*)

    I'm envious
    that you would rather talk to my wife
    than to me.

JUNIA. Really? If that is so, my lord,
    tell me what my crime was
    that you had to come and capture me
    in the middle of the night!
    You forced me here,
    so you surely know what I did
    to merit such treatment.

NERO. Is it not a state offense
    to have hidden from the emperor so long,
    to avoid any contact with him?
    These gifts of beauty
    that the Gods have bestowed on you,
    are they meant to be hidden?
    Or only from me?
    Are your charms to grow
    and your beauty to glow
    only where Britannicus may find
    and nourish them?
    You have shut me out of your life!
    You have banished me in my own court!
    Isn't that a crime?

    There are even rumors that,
    without my consent,
    you see Britannicus whenever he wishes
    and allow him to speak
    whatever is on his mind.
    It's hard for me to understand
    how you, so far removed from the emperor,
    are so accessible to Britannicus!
    And it's particularly hard
    that I've had to learn from others
    that you love him!

JUNIA. I will not deny, my lord,
    that he has not avoided a girl
    who is the last survivor of a famous family.
    In happier times,
    the emperor—your predecessor, Claudius—
    named me as the future bride
    of his son, Britannicus,

who has come to love me,
and not only because his father willed it.
And I must add that, at the time,
you and your mother willed it, too.
Of course, your wishes and hers
are always in accord.

NERO. My lady, my mother has her plans,
       and I have mine.
       But enough about Claudius and Agrippina!
       They have nothing to do now
       with how I think or feel or what I do.
       So let me come to the point.
       I intend to choose a husband for you.

JUNIA. Are you going to shame me
        by making a choice beneath me,
        one to disgrace my birth?
        I am descended from the Caesars, too!

NERO. No, my dear girl. No.
       The husband I have in mind
       would not bring disgrace to anyone.
       You have no need to fear that.

JUNIA. Well then, who is he, my lord?

NERO. (*Smiling.*) None other than I!

JUNIA. *You!*

NERO. I would, sweet girl, choose another,
       if I knew someone higher and better
       than Nero.

But I have looked over my court,
I have searched everywhere in Rome,
I have surveyed the entire empire,
and the more I looked the more I saw
that Caesar alone was worthy
of this precious treasure.
He dares not give it to anyone
other than the one to whom
Rome has entrusted the whole world!

Britannicus was expected to inherit the empire
at the time when Claudius chose him for you.
But this is another time.
The Gods have spoken,
and you must not defy the Gods.
They have chosen a different emperor
and a new love for you.
What good is it for me
to have my God-given glory
unless I also have you?
No one else will do to soothe my cares.
Only you.
You may wonder,
what cares has the emperor?
Do you think it's so easy to spend one's days
on the lookout for enemies?
Isn't it ironic that the whole world
envies the way the emperor spends his day
when they should be pitying him . . .
unless there are moments
when I may lie at your feet?

Do not let thoughts of Octavia
cast a pall over you.

Rome feels just as I do, repudiates Octavia,
and would have me dissolve this marriage
most assuredly not made in heaven.

My darling girl,
give consideration to this choice of husband,
who loves you and worships you,
who is smitten by your beautiful eyes,
and who offers you the universe.
Surely you cannot refuse.

JUNIA. My lord, I am astonished!
In the course of a single day,
you forced me to these precincts
as if I were a criminal;
and now, when I appear before you,
so frightened I even doubt my own innocence,
you suddenly offer me Octavia's place!
I do not deserve this honor—or this indignity!
Can you, my lord, hope
that a girl who has lost all her family
and who lives under a shadow of darkest grief
could suddenly enter
this dazzling world of splendor?
If the court's bright light shone on me,
it would only expose my crime
of robbing the rightful owner.

NERO. I've already told you!
I repudiate Octavia!
Consider the noble blood
from which you come,
and accept the glory of Caesar and empire.

Do not let fear or modesty
lead you to the glory of a refusal
(*Slowly and emphatically.*) you will regret!

JUNIA. My lord, I'm fully aware
of the magnitude of the gifts you offer,
but it would be criminal for me to accept.
The majesty belongs to another.

NERO. Your concern for my wife
is most touching.
She has in you a true friend. Hmm.
Well, I see that your mind is made up,
and nothing can change it.

But let there be no deception,
no hypocrisy.
The truth of the matter is
Octavia means less to you
than Britannicus!

JUNIA. Of course he matters to me!
I've made no attempt to hide it!
Although my sincerity may be indiscreet,
my lips always speak for my heart.
Not raised at court, I've never had
to measure my words
and become an expert in pretense.
I love Britannicus.
I was chosen for him at a time
when to marry him meant to marry the empire.
The very misfortune that cast him aside
has bound him even closer to me.

The emperor's days are spent in pleasure,
surrounded by countless people,
and the empire supplies his every want and need
abundantly and endlessly.
Britannicus is alone.
When he has troubles,
he has no one to turn to but me.
His pleasures are few, his cares are many,
and I alone wipe away his tears.

NERO. (*Wistfully.*) These are cares and tears
that Caesar envies.
Anyone else would pay for them with his life.
(*Sweetly.*) But your prince, my lady,
I am treating gently.
You will see him shortly.

JUNIA. (*Joyously.*) Ah, good lord,
I knew I could count on your better nature!

NERO. (*Continuing sweetly.*)
You know I could have prevented him
from ever seeing you again.
But I prefer not to incite his resentment,
for I do not want to ruin him.
I have decided . . .
he shall learn of his sentence . . .
(*Cruelly.*) from the lips of the one he loves.
(*Harshly commanding.*) If you value his life,
break with Britannicus now!
Say nothing of my jealousy!
Take all the blame for his banishment!
Tell him to take his love and hope elsewhere!

JUNIA. So! I must pronounce this heavy sentence,
    when my lips have sworn to him the opposite
    a thousand times!
    He'll never believe me.

NERO. (*Cruelly and inappropriately affectionately.*)
    Oh yes, he will!
    Lock your love
    in the deepest recesses of your soul!
    Do not let the least sign
    escape from your eyes,
    or he will be lost forever!

JUNIA. Don't make me do this!
    I have but one request, my lord.
    Never allow him to see me again!

NERO. No. It's too late for that.

NARCISSUS. (*Enters.*) My lord,
    Britannicus is on his way here.
    He is looking for the princess.

NERO. Let him come. I'm leaving.
    (*To* JUNIA.) His fate depends more on you
    than on me.
    Remember,
    I will be watching and listening
    to everything you say and do.

    (NERO *hides behind a column.* NARCISSUS *remains.*
    BRITANNICUS *runs in excitedly.*)

BRITANNICUS. Darling,
>What is this good fortune
>that brings me back to you?
>Can I truly enjoy
>this sweet moment with you?

>(*He tries to embrace and kiss* JUNIA, *but she firmly rebuffs him.*)

>(*Puzzled and fearful.*) Why,
>amid this pleasure,
>does anxiety suddenly grip my heart?
>Am I going to see you again?
>Will I have to sneak around to see you
>when we used to meet openly every day,
>and with so much happiness?
>Good Gods, what a night this has been—
>and what a morning!
>Your tears, your appearance
>have not moved these cruel bullies?
>Their insolence has not diminished at all?
>My darling, you say nothing!
>What a reception!
>What coldness!
>Speak!
>There's no one here but the two of us!
>Narcissus has seen to it
>that the enemy is occupied.
>Let's make the most of our time alone.

JUNIA. This is a place
>where he is all-powerful.
>The walls have eyes and ears.
>The emperor is never absent.

BRITANNICUS. Dearest,
> what makes you so fearful?
> Isn't it enough that you are held prisoner?
> Is your love held prisoner, too?
> Where is that heart that always swore
> to make even the emperor
> envious of our love?
> You have no cause to fear.
> Everyone seems to be on our side,
> even the emperor's mother.
> I'm told that Rome herself
> is offended by his conduct.

JUNIA. My lord,
> you don't know what you're saying!
> You yourself have told me a thousand times
> that Rome in one voice speaks Nero's praises.
> And you yourself
> have always paid tribute to his virtues.
> It must be your pain
> that makes you talk like this.

BRITANNICUS. Your words are astonishing!
> Did I come here to have him praised?
> I had to steal this moment
> to tell you of the grief that overwhelms me.
> And this precious moment is squandered
> by praising the enemy who persecutes me!
> The day has barely begun,
> and I hardly recognize you!
> Even your look says nothing.
> Your eyes dare not meet mine!
> What's happened?

Can it be
that now you love Nero and hate me?
In the name of the Gods,
explain this cruelty you inflict on me!
Tell me!
Have you forgotten me
completely?

JUNIA. Leave, my lord! Go!
   The emperor is coming.

BRITANNICUS. (*Turning to* NARCISSUS.)
   After such a blow, Narcissus,
   is there anyone I can trust?

   (BRITANNICUS *runs out.* NERO *slowly emerges from his hiding place.*)

NERO. My lady . . .

JUNIA. No, my lord!
   I can't listen to anything now!
   You have been obeyed.
   At least let me weep.
   He will not see my tears.
   (*Runs out, sobbing.*)

NERO. I had no idea
   that love could be so powerful!
   It even broke through her adamant silence.
   Well, she certainly loves him!
   I will enjoy making him give up hope!
   I will enjoy making him suffer!

With my own eyes,
I have seen him doubt his sweetheart's love.
I will run after Junia.
Narcissus, you run after Britannicus
and shatter him!
Torment him with new suspicions!
And while I am gazing on the tears
of the girl I adore,
make him pay dearly for the happiness
he doesn't even know is his!
(*Runs out, following* JUNIA.)

NARCISSUS. (*Aside.*)
So! Destiny calls on Narcissus again!
Who can resist her call?
I will follow her kind orders to the end!
(*Grins.*) Is there anything more delicious
than destroying those who suffer!
(*Runs out, following* BRITANNICUS.)

(*Fade-out.*)

Scene 3

TIME: *Morning.*

AT RISE: NERO *is playing his lyre.*

BURRUS. (*Enters and salutes.*) My lord,
　　your mother's adviser, Pallas,
　　has been banished.

NERO. (*Continues playing.*) How did she take it?

BURRUS. Not well. And you may be sure
　　she's on her way here now to scold you.
　　Her fury has long threatened to explode.
　　Let's hope it goes no further
　　than angry shouts and cries.

NERO. (*Stops playing.*) What do you mean?
　　Do you think
　　she's plotting something?

BURRUS. My lord, Agrippina
　　must always be feared.
　　Rome and the army worship her ancestors,
　　and they have great respect and admiration for her.
　　She is the daughter of Germanicus!
　　She is aware of her power,
　　and you know her courage.
　　What makes me fear her most, my lord,
　　is that when you provoke her,
　　you give her the ammunition
　　to use against you.

NERO. I, Burrus?

BURRUS. My lord,
    I have no better example
    than this new love that possesses you.

NERO. (*Resumes playing.*)
    There's no cure for it.
    I'm overwhelmed by it.
    My heart tells me more
    than anything you can say.
    I think of her constantly.
    This love is consuming me.

BURRUS. At this moment,
    you only imagine so.
    It is a sickness
    but only in its earliest stage.
    It can still be cured.
    But if you let it continue,
    it will grow and destroy you—
    for it will make you its slave.
    Turn your heart away
    from this illness
    now
    and direct it to your duty.
    Don't look for her,
    don't talk to her,
    don't see her.
    Think of the glory of your reign so far.
    And remember the things you once liked
    about Octavia—

(NERO *strums discordant notes.*)

her kindness, her beauty,
her sweet disposition, and her retiring ways.

(BURRUS *places a hand over the strings, preventing*
NERO *from playing. Then* BURRUS *removes his hand,*
w*hereupon* NERO *resumes strumming, even more dis-*
cordantly.)

She deserves better than this.
She still loves you deeply,
even though you scorn her.
Above all, avoid Junia.

(NERO *stops playing.*)

Don't let your eyes even catch a glimpse of her.
And believe me,
however much this love charms you now,
in a while it will be defeated and disappear.
One does not love unless one wants to.

NERO. (*Sternly.*) Burrus,
in all affairs of state and the Senate,
in all matters of war and peace,
I follow your advice.
But love is another thing.
I think you know nothing about it,
and I wouldn't want to punish you
for giving bad advice about something
of which you are ignorant.
(*Resumes playing, but now sweetly. Sighing.*)
I'm going to her now.
It's too hard for me to stay away.
(*Smiles, twirls, and exits.*)

BURRUS. Well, Burrus, you did not think
    you would have to deal with Nero in love!
    That makes things more difficult.
    Until now you've been able
    to hold this wild beast in check.
    But now it's about to break out of its cage!
    What atrocities will be unleashed?
    (*Turning toward heaven.*) O Jupiter, help me!

    (AGRIPPINA *enters with* ALBINA.)

AGRIPPINA. Well, Burrus,
    was I wrong in my suspicions?
    What excellent lessons
    you've been teaching your student!
    It seems that Nero's wife suddenly has a rival
    and that his marriage counts for nothing!
    And Pallas, my adviser, has been banished!
    Are you responsible for these things—
    you, the emperor's tutor,
    so famous for your lofty teachings,
    who takes such pride
    in keeping Nero's wild ways in check?
    A fine thing for a tutor to pander to his pupil
    rather than instruct him—
    you who always boasted
    how much you hated sycophants!
    Well, it seems you've become
    the worst one of them all,
    encouraging him to forget his wife
    and scorn his mother!

BURRUS. My lady, your accusations are unfair—
    and also premature!

So far the emperor has done nothing wrong.
He has exiled your minister,
who had only himself to blame.
This new matter is not beyond repair,
and the wellsprings of Octavia's tears
may soon dry up.
Calm your anger,
and bring Caesar back to her
through gentle ways.
Threats and shouts
will only make him wilder.

AGRIPPINA. Don't try to shut me up,
when my silence only provokes your scorn!
My son has tried to remove my power,
but heaven has left me enough
to avenge myself!
Britannicus has begun to show resentment
for crimes I committed—
to my regret—
years ago.
I intend to make it up to him.
I will bring him before the army;
in front of everyone,
I will tell how I wronged him.
And I will urge the army
to follow my example
and to atone for its crimes
as I intend to do for mine.
I will confess that all the rumors were true!
I come from a noble and renowned family,
one the army admires and respects.
Germanicus was my father!
The soldiers will pay attention to me

when I tell them by what treachery
Nero came to the throne,
which I acquired for him
through assassinations
and the banishment of innocents
and poisonings!
I will tell all!

BURRUS. My lady, they won't believe you.
As for my own participation—
I made the army pledge its loyalty to Nero.
For that I will not repent.
I did my duty—
what I thought was best
for the empire.
Claudius, by adopting Nero,
chose of his own free will
to give equal rights
to *your* son and *his* son.
And so, when Rome selected Nero,
Rome was acting justly.
Once Britannicus was passed over,
he had no further claim.
Nero's power rests on such a firm foundation
you cannot destroy it.
And if Nero takes the advice
I've given him today,
his kindness will make you unwilling
to uproot and overthrow him.
I leave you now, my lady.
I have duties to perform!
(*Bows and exits.*)

AGRIPPINA. (*To* ALBINA.)
>   If I do not bring Nero's new love to an end,
>   I am finished.
>   My place will be taken,
>   and I shall no longer count for anything.
>   Octavia's title is an empty one,
>   for she does nothing at court,
>   and she is ignored.
>   As for that other woman
>   who has captured Nero's affection,
>   whether as his wife or as his mistress,
>   *she will reign!*
>   She has but to cast a glance,
>   and she will be obeyed,
>   and I shall be discarded.
>   The fruit of all my labors
>   and the glory of all the Caesars—
>   *everything!*—
>   will become *hers,*
>   a prize for the woman he adores!
>   I cannot bear the thought of it!
>   Oh, Nero, ungrateful child!

(BRITANNICUS *enters with* NARCISSUS.)

BRITANNICUS. (*Excited.*) My lady,
>   our mutual enemy is not invincible.
>   There are many on our side.
>   Stirred by anger,
>   they agree there has been gross injustice.
>   I have been speaking to Narcissus.
>   He tells me that Nero is not yet in possession
>   of that selfish girl he loves
>   at my sister Octavia's expense.

He says that half the Senate sides with us.
But, my lady, as for you,
I can't really tell which side you're on.
I'm afraid you've managed my ruin too well
to count on any friends of mine.
I have none.
You turned them away from me
too meticulously.

AGRIPPINA. My lord, don't be so sure!
Everything now depends on our acting as one.
You have my full support, and you can count on it.
In spite of all your enemies,
I swear to you,
before all the Gods in heaven,
I will not go back on my word.
Nero in this matter is guilty,
but sooner or later he must listen to me.
I will try persuasion or force, whatever it takes.
And if I have to, I will take Nero's wife,
who is your sister and the daughter of Claudius,
with me
and tell the whole world
of her sorrow and my fear,
and thereby win everyone over.
Good-bye! It's all-out war against Caesar!

(NARCISSUS *is startled.*)

In the meantime, keep out of sight!

(BRITANNICUS *and* NARCISSUS *bow as* AGRIP-
PINA *and* ALBINA *exit.*)

BRITANNICUS. Narcissus,
    can I believe your story
    that Nero may not be able
    to divorce Octavia and wed Junia
    because half the Senate is against it?
    Or have you given me false hope?

NARCISSUS. What I've said is true,
    but this is not the place to talk about it.

BRITANNICUS. Well then,
    could you somehow, by your cunning,
    arrange for me to see . . .

NARCISSUS. Whom?

BRITANNICUS. I'm ashamed to tell you,
    but if you could do it,
    I'd be able to face
    whatever fate has in store for me.

NARCISSUS. I don't understand.
    After all the things she has done,
    you still love her
    and think that she loves you?

BRITANNICUS. No, Narcissus.
    And I know I should be angry at her,
    but in spite of myself, I'm not.
    I know I should blame her,
    but my heart forgives her—
    even invents excuses for her
    and her inexplicable behavior—
    and continues to worship her.

I can't believe anything bad of her,
hard as I try.
I know I should hate her,
but I can't bring myself all the way to hate—
only partially there.
I am *annoyed* with her.
Who could believe that her heart,
which appeared so noble,
and from her childhood
despised this untrustworthy court,
could, in the course of a single day,
cast away integrity
and work treachery unheard-of
even in a treacherous court?

NARCISSUS. Perhaps
she's been planning this victory
much longer than you think.
She knew a time would come
when the emperor would see
her beautiful eyes.
And so,
perhaps it was her strategy all along
to use haughtiness and aloofness
to catch him.

BRITANNICUS. Then I can't see her?
Is that what you're saying?

NARCISSUS. My lord, at this very moment,
she is listening to the solemn vows
of her new lover.

BRITANNICUS. Well, there's nothing more to say,
    so I may as well go. (*Starts to exit.*)

    (JUNIA *enters. She looks at* BRITANNICUS *and then*
    NARCISSUS. *Still fearful that* NERO *might be observ-*
    ing, JUNIA *does not embrace* BRITANNICUS. *Still*
    hurt by their previous encounter, he does not embrace
    her.)

    But look who's here, Narcissus!

NARCISSUS. (*Aside.*) Good Gods!
    I must run and tell the emperor!

    (*To* BRITANNICUS *and* JUNIA.)
    I know you two want to be alone. (*Exits.*)

JUNIA. You must leave the palace at once!
    Otherwise, you'll receive the brunt
    of the anger that I have aroused!
    Nero is furious!
    I was able to get away from him
    only because his mother came
    and distracted him.
    Go! Leave!
    And please don't speak badly of me.
    I will explain everything later.
    And remember this:
    you are always in my heart,
    and nothing can banish you.

BRITANNICUS. (*Angry.*) Oh, now I understand!
    My flight will give you what you want—
    is that it?

Will leave the field clear
for your new love?
No doubt, when you think of my humiliation,
you are delighted.
Well, I'll go.
(*Contemplative*.) It doesn't surprise me
that our love seems ordinary to you
now that you've been seduced by good fortune.
And it doesn't surprise me
that you're dazzled at the thought
of ruling this court at my sister's expense,
or that you're impressed—like everyone else—
with the splendor of the palace.
No. These things don't surprise me.
What surprises me is that, in the past,
you've always spoken
of the emptiness of such things.
I knew of the injustice built on my ruin,
and I knew that heaven itself
was a willing accomplice.
But I never expected that you, whom I adore,
would forsake me.
My desperate heart was prepared
for any disappointment but this.

JUNIA. One day, at a happier time,
     you will understand my strange behavior.
     But now you are in grave danger.
     So go quickly, before it's too late!
     My heart has not changed.
     Nero commanded me to pretend,
     and he was listening to every word we spoke.

BRITANNICUS. (*With the anger of realization.*)
    That . . . monster!

JUNIA. From his hiding place,
    he witnessed everything I said and did.
    He threatened to unleash
    terrible vengeance on you
    at any word or sign
    that we were communicating.

BRITANNICUS. So Nero was listening!
    Surely your eyes could have shown me
    that you were only pretending,
    but you hid them from me!
    One look from you—one only!—
    would have spared me all this pain!

JUNIA. If I wanted to save you,
    I couldn't let on.
    My heart wanted to blurt it out!
    How many sighs I had to stifle!
    How hard it was to avert my eyes,
    when they sought yours so forcefully!
    What torture for me to keep quiet,
    to hear you groan, and yet have to hurt you!
    And even so, I feared I betrayed myself—
    afraid I loved you so much
    there was no way I could hide it.
    I can't imagine what held back my tears.
    Nero knows too much about my heart and yours
    for his own good—and ours!
    Once again, go!
    You will hear more when we meet again.

BRITANNICUS. I already know too much!

(*They embrace and kiss passionately.*)

Oh, my dearest, my darling, my happiness!
What a criminal I was for doubting you!
You are so good!
Do you really understand
all that you're giving up for me?
How can I ever make it up to you?

JUNIA. By leaving at once!

(NERO *suddenly enters.*)

It's too late!

NERO. Please don't let me interrupt
this charming scene.
My lady, from the way he speaks to you,
I can only imagine the kindnesses
you must have showered on him.
He certainly should thank you—
but I think he owes me a bit of thanks, too,
for arranging this meeting place for you.

BRITANNICUS. Junia and I
can share our joys and sorrows
anywhere.

NERO. But isn't there something special
about this place
that tells you to show respect and obedience
to the emperor?

BRITANNICUS. You and I have known
    this place from childhood.
    There was nothing about it then
    that spoke of my obeying you
    and your lording over me.

NERO. Destiny once more
    has changed everything!
    You are such a boy! So young!
    Well, you can readily learn to obey,
    for the young are easy to teach!

BRITANNICUS. Who will be my teacher?

NERO. Rome.

BRITANNICUS. Does Rome give you the right
    of cruelty, injustice, force, violence, kidnapping,
    wanton imprisonment, whimsical divorce, terror?

NERO. Rome takes no notice
    of the things Caesar does in private.
    Imitate her respect!

BRITANNICUS. But Rome does have thoughts.

NERO. She does not speak them.
    Imitate her silence!

BRITANNICUS. So, Nero is beginning to show
    his true colors.

NERO. Nero is beginning to grow weary
    of your speeches.

BRITANNICUS. Every emperor
    ought to be remembered
    for the happiness of his reign.

NERO. Forget happiness!
    Think fear!

BRITANNICUS. Do you really believe
    such sentiments will please your beloved?

NERO. I may not know how to please her,
    but I certainly know how to punish
    a headstrong rival.
    Guards!

    (GUARDS *enter; one seizes* JUNIA, *the other seizes*
    BRITANNICUS.)

JUNIA. (*Struggling with the* GUARD; *to* NERO.)
    What are you doing? He is your brother!
    He has a thousand misfortunes!
    Can his one happiness make you so envious?

NERO. These men will escort you
    back to your separate apartments!

    (JUNIA *continues to struggle with her captors as she is
    led out, but* BRITANNICUS *does not struggle, and he
    and his* GUARD *do not move.*)

BRITANNICUS. (*To* NERO.)
    Nero, you certainly have a way with women!

NERO. (*To the* GUARD *in a rage*.) Guard,
    why are you still standing there?
    Get him out of my sight!

(*The* GUARD *seizes* BRITANNICUS *forcefully and
quickly exits with him.* NERO *gazes at the audience and
grins.*)

(*Fade-out.*)

INTERMISSION

ACT II

Scene 1

TIME: *Early afternoon.*

AT RISE: AGRIPPINA *is pacing anxiously.*   ALBINA
stands by a column, motionless.

BURRUS. (*Enters.*) My lady, the emperor agrees
    to give you a hearing.
    He's on his way here now.

AGRIPPINA. (*Angrily.*) He has placed me
    under house arrest
    and confined me to the palace!
    This is an outrage!

BURRUS. My advice to you
    is not to begin your audience
    by fuming and flying into a rage.
    It's true he's offended you,
    but don't begin by complaining of it.
    Rather, go to him as a mother,
    with open arms.
    As soon as he feels your mother love,
    he'll be receptive to you.
    Then you can defend yourself,
    but do not accuse him.
    Listen to his words,
    and let him explain his actions.

And always remember
that although he is your son—
your creation!—
he is still your emperor!
You are like us—
subject to the very power
you gave him.
But here he comes.
I'll go and leave you alone.

(NERO *enters and stops.* BURRUS *salutes him and exits.*)

AGRIPPINA. Come, dear,
give your mother a kiss.

(NERO *reluctantly kisses her.*)

Good. Now a hug.

(*They hug, he reluctantly.*)

(*Cheerily.*) All right, then.
Burrus says you intend to tell me
what I've done
for you to make me a prisoner.
(*Somewhat angrily.*)
Allow *me* to tell *you* the crime I've committed.
Allow *me* to enlighten *you*.
You reign, my darling! That is my crime!
Now I should like to remind you
how it came about that you are emperor.

NERO. Mother, I've heard the story
a thousand times!

AGRIPPINA. You apparently
      need to hear it again.

(*During* AGRIPPINA*'s speech,* NERO *exhibits adolescent boredom. He yawns, rolls and closes his eyes, lets
his jaw sag, wrinkles his brow, stretches, and even pre-
tends to climb a column.*)

AGRIPPINA. Britannicus's mother, Messalina,
      was condemned and executed for adultery.
      No sooner was she dead
      than many beautiful women—
      (*Smiling.*) myself included—
      began competing for her husband, Claudius.
      I was a widow with one son—you!
      I wanted Claudius for one reason only—
      to place my son on the throne!
      I went to visit Claudius every day,
      and each time he kissed me more tenderly.
      I knew he was falling in love.
      Although I was Claudius's niece,
      the Senate could find no Roman law
      prohibiting a niece from marrying an uncle.
      So I married him.
      There I was—the emperor in my bed
      and Rome at my feet.
      That did much for me, but nothing for you.
      But it was a good beginning!

NERO. Oh, Mother!

AGRIPPINA. Octavia, Claudius's daughter,
      was already engaged to Silanus, Junia's brother,
      when I decided she belonged to you.

So I broke the engagement,
and she married you.
That made you the emperor's son-in-law.
My plan was progressing!

Unfortunately, Silanus,
distraught and depressed
over the broken engagement,
killed himself.
Don't blame that on me!
Silanus did it! Not I!

NERO. Silanus killed himself
    because he didn't get Octavia.
    I'm ready to kill myself because I did!

AGRIPPINA. (*Ignoring him.*)
    Then I persuaded Claudius
    to adopt you as his son,
    equal with Britannicus.
    Claudius had become so fond of you
    he did it readily.
    Supporters of Britannicus
    could see where that was going
    and tried to stop it.
    But the emperor was worn down by me.

NERO. Really?

AGRIPPINA. (*Ignoring him.*)
    I was able to bribe by lavish gifts
    most of the supporters of Britannicus.
    And those who refused—the most seditious!—
    were sent into exile.
    Things were moving along!

Then I hired tutors for you,
worthy men, highly esteemed,
untouched by intrigue—
men who could be trusted—
one a man of letters, Seneca,
and the other a general in the army,
our dear Burrus.

To gain the people's support,
I used Claudius's wealth.
I ordered shows and circuses
and distributed bread and sweet cakes
to the mobs—
irresistible bait to win their hearts.

Then Claudius chose you as his successor.
Victory was now within my grasp!

(*To* ALBINA.) Albina, I'm thirsty.
Bring us something to drink—
a little wine mixed with water.

(ALBINA *exits*.)

As fate would have it,
Claudius became sick
and realized he'd made a mistake.
Until then he had been blind to me.
Suddenly he could see!
As he lay dying,
he murmured his own son's name
over and over again.
(*Gleefully*.) Too late!
His palace was mine!
His bed was mine!

His friends were mine!
His guards were mine!
I was determined that no one
should hear his last words—
"Britannicus! Britannicus!"—
and that Claudius should know nothing
of his son's tears.
I barred the son from his father's room
on the pretense that he was too young
to watch his father die.
All alone with Claudius,
I gave him a drug to speed him on his way.
He died, but I told no one—
not yet.

(ALBINA *enters carrying a silver cup, which she gives
to* AGRIPPINA, *who passes it to* NERO. *He looks at it
suspiciously, then passes it back to* AGRIPPINA, *who
looks at him quizzically. Then, understanding, she
quickly gulps some down, swallowing hard, then stops,
broadly smiles at* NERO, *and passes it back to him. He
readily drinks the remainder and gives the cup back to*
ALBINA, *who sets it down.*)

AGRIPPINA. I then sent you with Burrus to the army camp
to have the soldiers swear allegiance to you.
You marched by them smiling, waving,
and exchanging pleasantries.
Soldiers like that!
All the while, throughout Rome,
the altars smoked with sacrifices,
and the people prayed for the emperor's recovery.
Only when the legions had pledged their loyalty to you
did I announce that the emperor was dead
and that you were the new emperor.

Rumors flew that I'd poisoned him.
But how can anyone call "poison"
something that puts a dying man
out of his misery?

I achieved my goal!
Nero—my son!—was now the emperor.
Victory!
And I did it all by myself!
(*Announcing and saluting.*)
Hail, Caesar! Hail, Caesar!

Well, my *grateful* son!
Those are the crimes I committed for you.
And now, house arrest is my reward!

NERO. Mother . . .

AGRIPPINA. I'm not finished yet!
Yesterday I promised Junia to Britannicus,
and what did you do but kidnap Junia
and carry her off to court,
where she suddenly became
the object of your affection,
your wife erased from your heart!
Then my minister and adviser, Pallas,
whom you imagined turned me away from you
and toward Britannicus,
was banished and sent into exile!
Then you imprisoned me!
And I've just heard
that Britannicus has been arrested!
You have acted so shamefully
that you should have come
on bended knee to *me*

to explain your crimes to *me*!
Instead, you order me here
to explain myself to *you*!

NERO. Mother, I've never forgotten
that I owe the empire to you.
But everyone believes you did it
only for yourself.
People say, "Did she crown him
so he would obey her?"
And "Is he but the reservoir of her power?"
Even in the Senate they are saying,
"When the emperor opens his mouth,
it is his mother who speaks!"

That angers the people, who think I am weak
and call me your puppet.
And it enrages the soldiers
who carry the eagles and the standards,
symbols of past Roman glory,
in front of your sedan.
(*Angrily.*) My lady, Rome wants a master,
not a mistress!

And what is this latest rumor I hear,
that you've joined forces with Britannicus?
By arranging his marriage to Junia,
you further reinforce your strength.
And Pallas, your cunning adviser,
advises you on how to accomplish these things.
So many intrigues, Mother!

(*Wounded.*) I hear you're even planning
to parade Britannicus before the army,
as you once did me.

(*Pleading.*) Don't I have the right
to protect myself against such outrages?
But when I do, you become angry with me.

AGRIPPINA. So that's why you arrested me!
    Whom are you listening to?
    I make Britannicus the emperor?
    How can you believe that?
    Why should I do that?
    What honors could I hope for at his court?
    The first thing they'd do is condemn me
    for crimes I committed on your behalf.
    And I would be convicted, then executed!

    You cannot deceive me, you scoundrel!
    You were ungrateful even as a little boy.
    And my care and affection meant nothing.
    Your hugs and kisses were pretenses.
    Oh, you were clever and you were hard.
    Your nature should have stopped my kindnesses
    in their tracks! (*Weeping.*)
    Oh, how unhappy I am!
    I have only one son,
    and look how he treats me!

    Have I ever done anything
    that wasn't for you?
    As the Gods are my witnesses,
    have I ever offered prayers or made vows
    that weren't for you?
    How many times have I had to endure
    scorn, guilt, fear, and danger?
    But none of these could stop me
    where my child was concerned.

I did what had to be done
to place you where you are.
You are the emperor!

But enough of this.
My lord, you have deprived me of my liberty.
Why don't you take my life, too,
if that is your wish?
The fortune-tellers long ago foretold that.
And I said to them, "Let him kill me—
so long as he is emperor!"

(BURRUS *enters and observes, but they pay no attention to him.*)

NERO. (*Shaking his head despairingly.*)
Mother, Mother, Mother!
Just tell me what you want.

AGRIPPINA. I want my accusers punished!
I want the anger of Britannicus appeased!
I want Junia to be allowed
to take the husband of her choice!
I want both of them set free!
I want my adviser, Pallas, recalled from exile!
And I want the emperor
to allow his mother to see him
whenever she wishes!

NERO. My lady, as a token
of my eternal gratitude,
I shall henceforth engrave your power
on every heart!
The cold chill between us
has turned out well,

for it has rekindled our old mutual love.
I'll give you everything you ask for,
and I'll even reconcile myself with Britannicus.
As for that girl and my love for her,
which has been the principal cause
of our estrangement,
whatever you decide will be done.

You may go now and bear the good news
to Britannicus, my brother.

AGRIPPINA. (*Throwing her arms around Nero
and hugging and kissing him.*)
Oh, my darling Nero!

(AGRIPPINA *and* ALBINA *exit;* BURRUS *salutes as
they go.*)

BURRUS. My lord, this reconciliation
between your mother and you is wonderful.
It will make everyone happy.
You know I've never said a bad word about her,
and I've never tried to drive a wedge
between the two of you,
so I don't understand your anger toward me.

NERO. Well, Burrus, I thought both of you
were against me,
but her open hostility toward you
makes me trust you again.
However,
my mother is too quick to claim victory.
For it is my intention, regarding Britannicus,
to embrace him *only to strangle him!*

BURRUS. My lord! What are you saying?

NERO. Things have gone too far, Burrus.
　　　Britannicus must die!
　　　Nothing else will release me
　　　from my mother's madness.
　　　As long as he lives,
　　　I am only half alive.
　　　I have grown weary
　　　of hearing my mother speak his name.
　　　I do not intend to let her audacity
　　　continue to promise him my place.

BURRUS. You're serious.
　　　You really mean to kill him.

NERO. Before the day ends.

BURRUS. But why, my lord, why?

NERO. To preserve my glory,
　　　my love, my safety, my life.

BURRUS. This reckless plan
　　　is not your doing.
　　　I can't believe it is your idea.
　　　You can't mean it!
　　　How can you listen to yourself
　　　without shuddering?
　　　Have you considered whose blood it is
　　　you mean to spill and bathe in?
　　　Is Nero bored with the people's love?
　　　Have you considered
　　　what they'll say about you?

NERO. Am I to think only
        of my reputation?
        Should I submit to every desire
        but my own?
        Be emperor just to please others?
        Am I not entitled to please myself?
        What about this love
        that chance has just given to me?
        Is it to be snatched away
        on the very same day?

BURRUS. Is it not pleasure enough
        to have the people's love?
        Until now you have been virtuous,
        and you always can be.
        It's up to you.
        You are still master.
        Is there anything better for a leader
        than going from one good deed to another?

        If you follow the advice
        of those who pander to you,
        you will be driven from crime to crime.
        Cruelty will be piled on cruelty,
        and you will dip your hands
        ever more deeply in blood.
        The death of Britannicus
        will agitate his supporters,
        and they will avenge him.
        And these avengers
        will bring forth even more.
        And after all the current ones are slain,
        successors will follow.
        My lord, you are lighting a fire
        that can never be put out!

Once you are feared,
you will always be feared,
not only by the court
but by the whole world.
Forever finding victims,
you will never be safe.
And you will regard all your subjects
as enemies.

Does the greatness of your first years
make you despise them?
Look at all the happiness
you've brought to Rome!
Is there anything more pleasurable
than that?
You, Caesar, are able to say:
"Everywhere at this moment,
I am loved.
The people do not start when they hear my name.
The Gods do not think of me and weep.
No hostile looks follow my appearance.
All hearts are light as I go by."
How many emperors could say that?
And you want to change it?

O Gods in heaven!
The poorest man's blood
was precious to you once.
Don't you remember that day in the Senate
when you were asked to sign
a guilty man's death warrant?
You resisted. You said,
"The sentence is too severe, too cruel.
Do you think that Nero has no feelings?"
That, my lord, is an emperor!

ACT II BRITANNICUS

If you do not wish to follow my advice,
then I'm afraid
my own death is the only remedy
to spare me the pain of this catastrophe.
I cannot go on living if you are intent
on taking so grisly an action.
My lord, send for the executioner,
for I can never consent
to what you are planning!
Call those cruel men
who've put you up to this
and have them slay me!
Name those traitors who advise you
to murder an innocent brother!

NERO. (*In anguish.*) Burrus, tell me
what you would have me do.

BURRUS. My lord,
Britannicus doesn't hate you.
I don't think he's capable of hating anyone.
He is innocent.
I will answer to you for his obedience.
Let me arrange a meeting
between the two of you.
You'll see how pleasant that will be.

NERO. Go and do it!

(BURRUS *exits as* NARCISSUS *enters. They nod
to each other icily.*)

NARCISSUS. My lord, I have prepared everything.
The poison is ready, and it's highly effective.
It's been tested.

NERO. Tested? On a goat . . . or a pig?

NARCISSUS. No, my lord.
    The only reliable test is on a man.
    So we gave it to a slave.
    He died instantly!

NERO. Well done, Narcissus!
    But put it aside for now.
    Britannicus and I are to be reconciled.

NARCISSUS. (*Astonished.*) Far be it from me
    to tell the emperor what to do,
    but do you know what you are doing?
    Today Britannicus was arrested.
    Do you think he'll ever forget that?
    And in time,
    everything hidden will come to light.
    One day he'll learn
    that on your orders
    I prepared poison for him.
    And then he may do
    the very thing you dare not do.

NERO. No, Narcissus,
    his heart is too good.
    I will try to conquer mine.

NARCISSUS. What about your love for Junia?
    Are you giving that up for him, too?

NERO. (*Angrily.*) Narcissus, you're going too far!
    Whatever may come of this,
    Britannicus is not my enemy.

NARCISSUS. Agrippina swore she'd take control again,
    and I see she has.

NERO. What do you mean?

NARCISSUS. She boasted about it in court.

NERO. She boasted about what?

NARCISSUS. She said
    that all she needed to do was speak with you,
    and you would be happy to make peace with her—
    that she would forget everything you've done,
    and you would be greatly relieved
    when she forgave you.

NERO. (*In anguish.*) Narcissus, tell me
    what you want me to do.
    Believe me, Narcissus,
    there's nothing I want more
    than to get rid of Britannicus.
    But wouldn't such an act
    be followed by eternal regret?
    And what would the whole world say?
    Would you have me follow the tyrant's path?
    Would you have Rome take away
    all my titles but one—*Assassin*?

NARCISSUS. My lord, what do you care
    what the world says?
    Let Britannicus die,
    and let Octavia be discarded
    according to your wishes.
    Do you listen to everyone but yourself?
    You do not know the Romans.

They worship the man who holds them in his power.
If you are too timid,
the Romans will think you fear them.
The Romans love to pile victims on the altar.
Even if they are innocent, you can be sure
the Romans will find crimes for them.

Those who advise you to spare Britannicus
are only looking out for themselves.
They know that if you kill him,
their influence in court is over.
But if you spare Britannicus, people will say:
"Nero was not born for empire.
He only does what his mother and others
tell him to do.
All he really cares about is riding horses,
driving chariots,
making a spectacle of himself
in front of the Romans
by competing for prizes unworthy of him,
or singing songs upon the stage,
or reciting his own poetry,
which he thinks are masterpieces,
all the while soldiers in the theater
are prompting the audience to shout
'Bravo!' and 'Encore!'
and to applaud enthusiastically."
My lord, don't you want to change this image?

NERO. (*Stunned and almost in tears.*)
　　Narcissus, I need some time to think about this!

　　(NERO *runs out.* NARCISSUS *remains and grins.*)

　　　　　　　(*Fade-out.*)

Scene 2

TIME: *Late afternoon.*

AT RISE: BRITANNICUS *and* JUNIA *enter, conversing.*

BRITANNICUS. (*Excited, happy.*) Sweetheart,
do you realize what's happened?
Nero—who would have believed it?—
is waiting for me now with open arms
to make our reconciliation!
He says that his love for you,
which has caused so much enmity,
is over.
Although my ancestral rank is lost,
and he—not I—wears my father's crown,
he no longer stands in the way of our love.
My heart forgives him.
He is my older brother, after all.
And now I can delight in you,
who gave up emperor and empire
for me!

(*Studying* JUNIA*'s concerned face.*)

Oh, my darling! What's wrong?
What is this new fear that constrains your joy,
when I'm so happy?

JUNIA. I don't know, but I'm afraid.

BRITANNICUS. You still love me, don't you?

JUNIA. Oh yes, I love you. I adore you!

BRITANNICUS. Darling,
Nero no longer obstructs our happiness.

JUNIA. How can you be sure?
What makes you think he's sincere?
One moment he loves me
and swears to kill you.
The next moment he gives me up
and seeks your friendship.
Is such a change possible
in the blink of an eye?

BRITANNICUS. Agrippina did this.
She thought my ruin would be the end of her.
Thanks to her fears,
our enemies have become our friends.
I trust the joy she has brought me.
I trust Burrus.
Why, I even trust Nero.
Besides, I don't think he's capable of treachery
any more than I am. Nero either hates openly
or not at all.

JUNIA. Oh, Britannicus!
You must not judge another heart by yours.
His lips and heart are so far apart,
they never act as one.
In this court, they delight in treachery—
they take joy in breaking promises
and not keeping their word.
What a strange land for you and me.

BRITANNICUS. Well, just as you fear Nero,
don't you think Nero fears
the Senate and the People of Rome?

He realizes he's been unjust,
and he's sorry.
Even Narcissus saw that.

JUNIA. Oh yes, *Narcissus*!
Do you really think you can trust *him*?

BRITANNICUS. What makes you say that?

JUNIA. Your life is at stake!
I suspect everything and everyone.
Nothing is safe. No one can be trusted.
I fear Nero now more than ever.
I fear Misfortune, which always pursues me.
I'm filled with darkest foreboding,
and I'm afraid to let you out of my sight.
This reconciliation that means so much to you
may yet conceal a trap.
I fear for your life!
I fear (*Bursting into tears.*)
that I am speaking to you for the last time!

(*He takes her in his arms.*)

BRITANNICUS. Stop your weeping.
Let me wipe away your tears.
In this palace, where I'm shunned
and he's worshipped,
you prefer my wretched state to his splendor!
Your love exalts me higher than the emperor!
You gave up Rome for me!
Oh, my darling, stop weeping,
for even your tears are precious to me.
I'll return soon, and you'll see
that your fears are groundless.

(*They kiss passionately.*)

I must go now, or Nero will get upset.
I'm already late.
Good-bye. I go, my heart filled with love.
Good-bye.

(*He starts to run off.*)

JUNIA. Britannicus!

BRITANNICUS. (*Stopping and turning.*)
    They are waiting! I must go!

(AGRIPPINA *enters.*)

AGRIPPINA. Why are you still here, Britannicus?
    You're late!
    Go at once!
    Nero's complaining that you're delaying
    that special moment when the two of you
    make up and embrace
    and the court explodes in joy.
    Don't let this precious feeling grow cold!

BRITANNICUS. My lady,
    I can't thank you enough for all your help.
    And my dearest Junia, love of my life,
    rest assured,
    I will come back to you as soon as I can!

AGRIPPINA. Yes! But go, Britannicus.
    Go!

(*He runs off. She turns to* JUNIA.)

My dear, what's troubling you?
I can see you've been weeping.

JUNIA. I can hardly believe
the transformation in your son.
It's a miracle!
But change is common at court.
And love, like any form of happiness,
can never be entirely carefree.

AGRIPPINA. My dear, all is well.
I've spoken to him, and he's changed.
Trust me!
There's no room for doubt
regarding the peace that I have brought about.
Nero has made pledges never to be broken.
Had you only seen how tenderly
he caressed and kissed me
as he renewed the promises he'd made.
I started to leave,
but his arms would not let me go.
His kindness shone like the sun.
He poured out his heart
like a little boy resting his head on his mother's breast.
Then he put on a severe countenance
to show that he was the emperor
consulting with his mother
and making decisions
that decide the fate of men.

Oh no, my dear!
We must declare his glory!
His heart has no trace of darkness or malice!
It is our enemies who turn him against us!

(*Radiantly.*) But now,
as their power is diminishing,
(*Triumphantly.*) Rome
will have Agrippina back again!

(*Faint distant shouting.*)

Why, they adore me so,
I can already hear their shouts!
Come! Let us visit Octavia,
and tell her how this day,
which began so ominously,
has ended so beautifully!

(*Loud distant shouting.*)

What is that shouting? What's happening?

JUNIA. O Gods in heaven, save my beloved!

(BURRUS *enters running breathlessly and continues across the stage.*)

AGRIPPINA. Burrus, stop!
Why are you running?

(BURRUS *stops.*)

What's happened?

BURRUS. My lady, it's done!
Britannicus is dying.

JUNIA. (*Wailing.*) Oh, my love, my all!

AGRIPPINA. Dying?

BURRUS. No. Britannicus is dead.

JUNIA. I'm going to save him if I can.
    And if I can't, I will follow him!
    (*Running off, sobbing.*)

BURRUS. It's my end, too. I cannot survive.
    I must leave this court
    and this emperor!

AGRIPPINA.   What happened?
    Tell me everything!

BURRUS. It began well enough.
    Most of the court had already assembled,
    happy in anticipation
    of the reconciliation.
    Britannicus came running into the room,
    apologizing for being late.
    The emperor, all forgiving,
    rose to embrace him.

    Then two silver cups were brought forth,
    one placed in the hand of Nero,
    the other in that of Britannicus.
    Narcissus filled the cups.
    Nero lifted his to make the first toast:
    "I call upon the Gods to look favorably
    on this happy day of reconciliation
    between Nero and Britannicus."
    Then Britannicus made his toast,
    the same as Nero's.
    Britannicus lifted his cup;

his lips had barely touched the rim—
no sword could have worked more swiftly!—
when the light went out from his eyes,
and he fell lifeless to the floor.

Nero showed no trace of astonishment.
He said, "It's nothing. Only a fit.
He often had them in childhood.
It seems violent
but presents no danger."
And so, watching him die, he just stood there,
his face not changing color,
indifference in his eyes—
the countenance of a tyrant.
Narcissus tried to look concerned, but in vain;
he could not help showing his joy.
Forcing myself through the crowd,
I ran from the room
to mourn Britannicus . . .
Caesar . . .
and Rome.

(NERO *and* NARCISSUS *enter.*)

NERO. (*Affecting distress.*) O great Jove!

AGRIPPINA. Oh, stop it, Nero!
    Britannicus is dead!
    Murdered!
    And I know who did it!

NERO. *Who*, my lady?

AGRIPPINA. *You!*

NERO. *Me?* Oh, Mother,
   you suspect me of everything!
   Any time there's trouble,
   I'm always to blame!
   To listen to you, my lady,
   it was I who put an end to Claudius!
   Mother, I know how much you loved Britannicus,
   and I have no doubt his death
   comes as a terrible shock,
   but I am not responsible
   for sudden quirks of fate.

AGRIPPINA. Liar!
   Britannicus was poisoned.
   Narcissus did it, but you ordered it.

NERO. Mother, what makes you say
   such a terrible thing?

NARCISSUS. (*To* NERO.) Agrippina's accusation
   is not outrageous.

   (NERO *becomes agitated.* NARCISSUS *speaks to*
   AGRIPPINA.)

   My lady, Britannicus had secret designs
   that would have given you cause for regret.
   He aimed for more than marriage with Junia.
   He would have punished you for your kindness.
   He was deceiving you.

   Britannicus was deeply resentful
   and would have done anything
   to restore his past glory.

Sooner or later, his injured heart
would have acted on his resentment.
The emperor relied on me to deal with him.
So, does it really matter
whether Fate or Narcissus
has served you?

AGRIPPINA. Nero,
continue to surround yourself
with ministers like this one,
and you will be able to boast
of many more glorious deeds!

You have begun
by shedding your brother's blood.
I can see what's coming next.
You will strike your mother.
You hate me
and resent all the good things
I've done for you.

But no good will come of my death.
I have given you everything—
the sky above,
the earth beneath your feet,
the light of day,
Rome.
So if you kill me,
I'll never leave you alone!
My face will appear everywhere
before your eyes,
and guilt like the Furies
will follow you!

You will try to calm your terror
by committing new atrocities.
Day after day new blood will flow.
And your madness will only increase
as you wallow ever deeper in blood,
until the Gods—at last grown weary—
will add one final victim
to your others—*you!*

Yes, you will end up killing yourself!
And your name will be such
to future generations
that the cruelest of tyrants,
if compared with you,
will consider it an insult!

That is my prophecy for you.
I have nothing more to say.
Good-bye.
Go.
Leave me alone.

(NERO *scowls at* AGRIPPINA.)

NERO. (*Furiously.*) Narcissus, follow me!

(NERO *exits, followed by* NARCISSUS. BURRUS *remains, facing* AGRIPPINA, *his eyes filled with tears.* AGRIPPINA *stands immobile, devastated and weeping.*)

(*Fade-out.*)

Scene 3

TIME: *Evening.*

AT RISE: GUARDS *enter, light the torch lamps, and exit.*
    AGRIPPINA *is in profound grief.* BURRUS *has re-*
    sumed his soldier's bearing.

AGRIPPINA. Burrus,
    nothing can stop him now!
    Did you see the furious look
    he gave me as he left?
    A monster is on the loose.
    I am next—or you.
    It's all over for us.

BURRUS. My lady,
    I've lived one day too long.
    I wish he had killed me
    before Britannicus.
    I can no longer bear him.
    It is not only his crime
    that has shattered me,
    but the coldness and ruthlessness
    in his eyes—present since childhood.
    I have no wish to escape now.
    Let him put me to death
    as quickly as possible.

ALBINA. (*Enters.*) My lady, my lord,
    you must run to the emperor at once!
    You must save him from his madness!
    He is forever separated from Junia!

AGRIPPINA. (*Fearful and concerned.*) Is she dead?

ALBINA. No. Dead only to Nero.
    Alive to everyone else.
    She pretended she was running to Octavia
    to tell her what had happened,
    but she took the secret passages and escaped.
    She ran out the palace gates like a mad woman.
    I followed her.
    When she came to the marble statue
    of Caesar Augustus in the plaza,
    she threw her arms around the legs.
    Weeping upon the feet,
    she cried: "O Prince, great Emperor,
    look with favor on this remnant of your family!
    Within your palace,
    Rome itself has just been sacrificed—
    Britannicus—
    the last surviving prince to resemble you."

    Then she took out a dagger hidden in her cloak
    and was just about to stab herself
    when some women standing nearby grabbed her,
    snatched the weapon from her hands,
    lifted her from the statue,
    embraced her, and tried to comfort her.
    The populace,
    amazed at the sight and touched by her tears,
    darted from all sides and crowded round
    to protect her.
    The women who had saved her
    led her to the temple of Vesta,
    Goddess of the hearth and home,
    where dedicated virgins faithfully keep alive
    their precious charge—
    the flame that burns eternally
    in honor of the Gods.

Nero saw everything
but dared not intervene,
for the sanctuary is inviolate.

Narcissus was bolder.
To please the emperor,
he ran to Junia
to stop her from climbing
the steps to the temple
and laid defiled hands on her;
but the crowd,
understanding everything,
dealt him countless mortal blows
with Junia's dagger.
His sacrilegious blood poured out
at the foot of the temple steps.

Caesar returned to the palace
wild-eyed and silent—
his appearance so terrifying
that everyone was afraid to go near him.
I think I heard him cry one word only—
(*Softly*.) "Junia!"

My lady, go to him.
If he is left alone,
without your help
and overwhelmed by grief,
he will surely kill himself.
Time is of the essence!
So hurry,
lest, on a sudden impulse,
he destroy himself!

AGRIPPINA. As well he should!
    (*Reconsidering.*) But I'm his mother—
    and he needs me now.
    Perhaps remorse
    will bring about a change in him.

BURRUS. May it please the Gods
    that this be the last of his crimes!

(*Fade-out.*)

THE END

THE PLAYWRIGHT

Howard Rubenstein is a physician and a writer. He was born in 1931 in Chicago and received a B.A. from Carleton College in 1953 and an M.D. from Harvard Medical School in 1957. In 1967 he was appointed Physician and Chief of Allergy at the Harvard University Health Services. In 1989 he became a medical consultant to the Department of Social Services, State of California. In 2000 he retired from the practice of medicine.

Rubenstein's translation of Aeschylus' *Agamemnon* was produced by Granite Hills Acting Workshop (GHAW), El Cajon, California, in 1997. A videotape of a performance of that production was requested by Oliver Taplin, Regius Professor, Oxford, and may be found in the Archive of Performances of Greek and Roman Drama, University of Oxford, England. Rubenstein translated and adapted Euripides' *The Trojan Women*, which was produced by GHAW in 2001. That production was the most decorated show, professional or amateur, of the 2001 San Diego theater season (*San Diego Playbill*).

Rubenstein's *Brothers All*, a play based on *The Brothers Karamazov* by Dostoyevsky; and *The Golem, Man of Earth*, a play based on H. Leivick's Yiddish dramatic poem *The Golem*, had their premieres at 6th@Penn Theatre in San Diego in 2006.

Rubenstein's *Tony and Cleo*, a play based on historical sources, about the love affair of Antony and Cleopatra, had its premiere at 6th@Penn Theatre in 2008. It was the most successful off-night (Sundays through Wednesdays) production in that theater's history.

Howard Rubenstein has also written *Maccabee*, an epic in free verse.